Creating with Cardboard

By Amy Quinn

CHERRY LAKE
Publishing

Published in the United States of America by
Cherry Lake Publishing
Ann Arbor, Michigan
www.cherrylakepublishing.com

Series Editor: Kristin Fontichiaro
Photo Credits: Cover, davidd / tinyurl.com/zx4kjyp /
CC BY 2.0; all other images by Amy Quinn

Library of Congress Cataloging-in-Publication Data
Names: Quinn, Amy, 1976– author.
Title: Creating with cardboard / by Amy Quinn.
Description: Ann Arbor, Michigan : Cherry Lake Publishing, [2018] | Series:
    Makers as innovators junior | Audience: K to grade 3. | Includes
    bibliographical references and index.
Identifiers: LCCN 2017004420| ISBN 9781634726931 (lib. bdg.) | ISBN
    9781634727266 (pbk.) | ISBN 9781634727594 (pdf) | ISBN 9781634727921
    (ebook)
Subjects: LCSH: Cardboard art—Juvenile literature. | Handicraft—Juvenile
    literature.
Classification: LCC TT870 .Q46 2018 | DDC 745.5—dc23 LC record available at
    https://lccn.loc.gov/2017004420

Cherry Lake Publishing would like to acknowledge the work of the Partnership for
21st Century Learning. Please visit *www.p21.org* for more information.

Printed in the United States of America
Corporate Graphics

A Note to Adults: Please review the instructions for the activities in this book before allowing children to do them. Be sure to help them with any activities you do not think they can safely complete on their own.

A Note to Kids: Be sure to ask an adult for help with these activities when you need it. Always put your safety first!

Table of Contents

Old boxes, tubes, and other cardboard items can be recycled into games, toys, art, and more!

Introduction

Have you ever wanted to create your own game, toy, or other invention? You might be a **maker**! Cardboard is one of the easiest materials that makers can use to build things. You can use cardboard to design your project just the way you want. This book will show you how to make your own cardboard creations.

Gather all of the supplies you need before you get started.

Materials

Here are some things you'll need:

- Cardboard boxes in a variety of sizes
- Scissors or box cutters
- Tape
- Hot glue gun
- Markers
- Ruler
- Art scraps

Safety Tips

Always ask an adult to help you with sharp objects or a hot glue gun. These tools are useful, but they can be very dangerous.

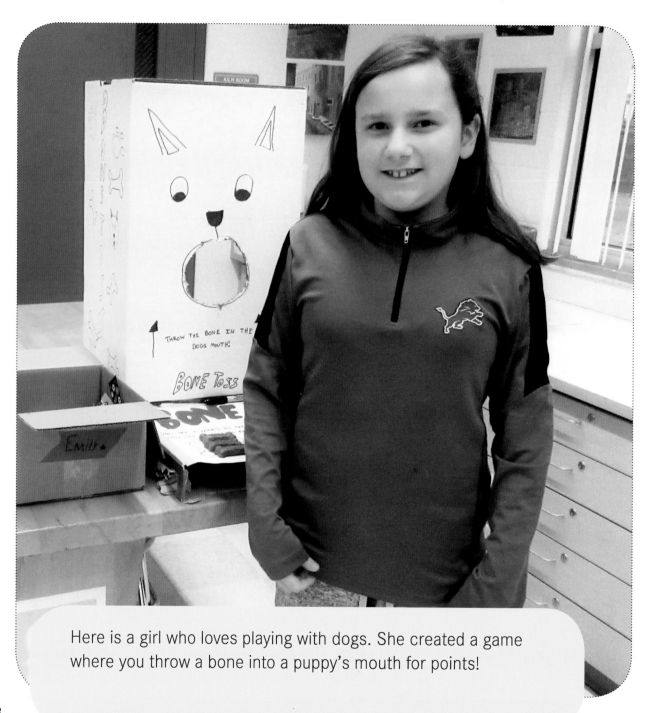

Here is a girl who loves playing with dogs. She created a game where you throw a bone into a puppy's mouth for points!

Imagine an Idea

To get started, you'll need an idea for something to make. Every great invention starts with a good idea. Think of games you enjoy. Think of the toys kids like to play with. Use your imagination to think of a new toy you can create out of cardboard.

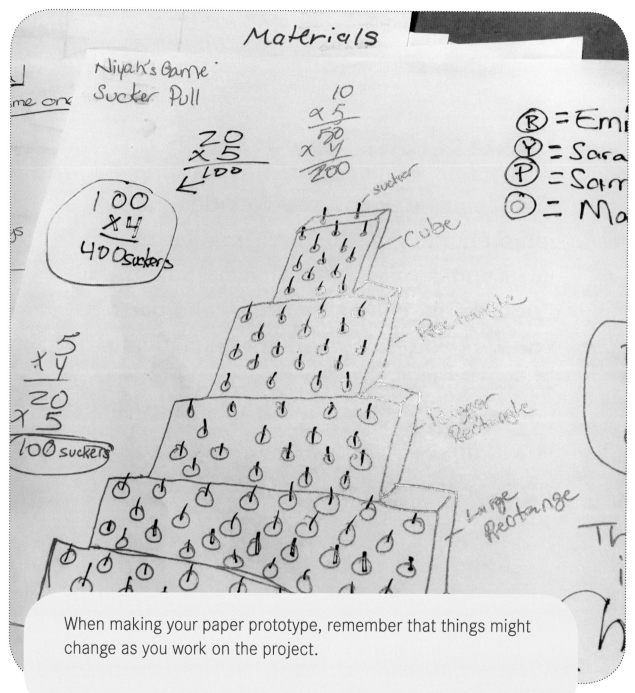

When making your paper prototype, remember that things might change as you work on the project.

Cardboard Engineer

Engineers are people who design and build things. You will be an engineer who uses cardboard to design something useful. Begin by sketching a **prototype** of what you are going to create on a piece of paper. This will help you plan what size and shape you need your boxes to be. It will also allow you to figure out if any other materials will be helpful.

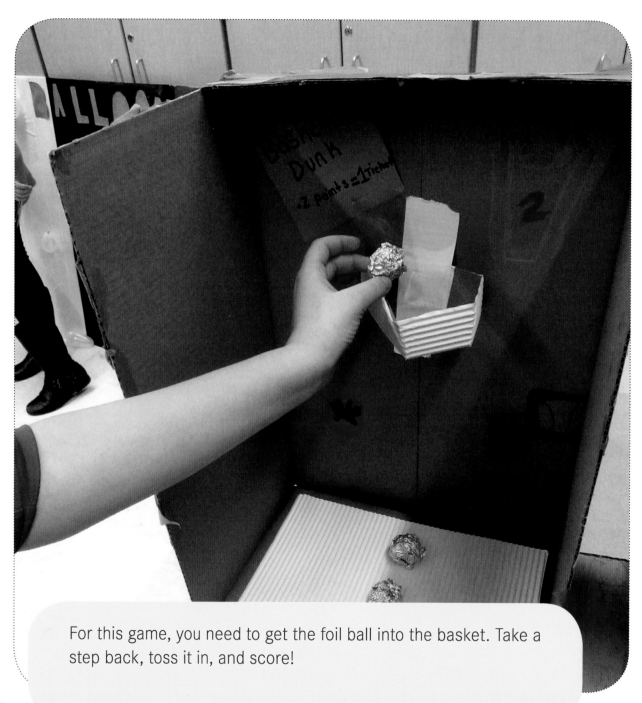

For this game, you need to get the foil ball into the basket. Take a step back, toss it in, and score!

Make a Game

Let's make a game board. Cut cardboard to the size and shape you want. You can tape cardboard pieces together if you need to. Use paper, paint, or markers to decorate it. Add details such as a game name, game pieces, and rules. Then test your game with friends. Improve it so it is just right!

Know Your Audience

Think of who is going to play your game. What can you do to make it more challenging or fun for all ages? What do they need to do to win the game?

Do you like playing with toy cars? Create a town for your cars to zoom around!

Make a Toy

Now try making a toy. Use your plan to figure out what materials you will need. Start with the biggest box and add smaller parts by taping or gluing them on. Think of what colors or materials you can add to make your creation just right. Test your toy by playing with it. Make changes and improve your toy as needed.

Making your own storage bin allows you to organize your items just the way you like them.

Make a Storage Bin

If you are making a cardboard storage bin, first think of what needs organizing. Take a look around. Do you have any toys, art supplies, building materials, or even stuffed animals that need to be organized? Cut the cardboard to the size and shape you need. Then have fun decorating it!

Take a Look

Something really useful you can make out of cardboard is a container for art supplies. By putting small boxes inside of a larger box, you can create a nice organized space. Take a look at this cool storage idea for art supplies made out of cardboard. Creating an organizer is very easy and helpful!

Try making cool art projects to decorate your room, then show them off to your friends.

Cardboard Celebration

Once your creation is ready, invite your friends and family to a cardboard celebration. They'll have fun playing with your games and toys. You can join in on the fun and celebrate being a cardboard engineer! You might even inspire someone else to create something special. Remind them that all they need to get started are an idea and some cardboard!

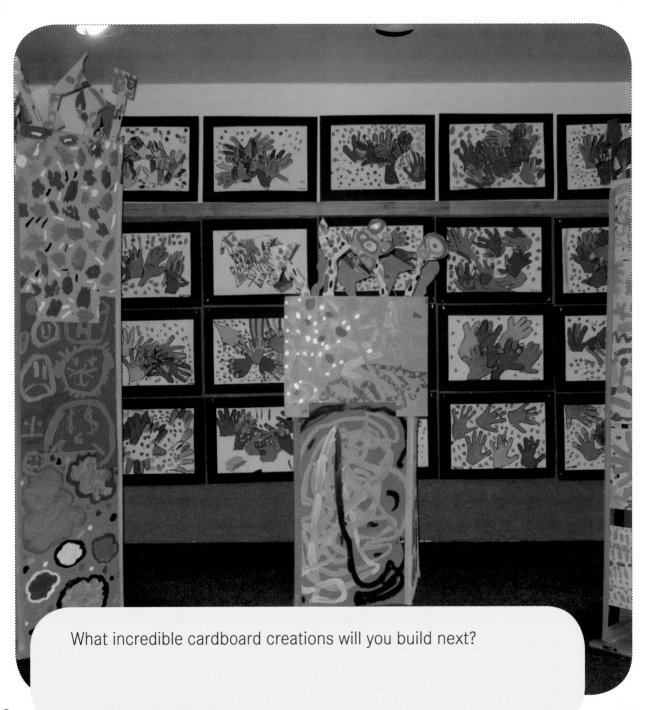

What incredible cardboard creations will you build next?

Wrapping Up

Creating and engineering with cardboard is fun and easy. Best of all, it gives old boxes a whole new use. Next time you see a cardboard box, don't throw it away! You can turn it into something amazing!

Glossary

engineers (en-juh-**NEERZ**) people who use knowledge of science, math, and technology to design and build solutions to practical problems

maker (**MAY**-kur) person who likes to design, build, and tinker with everything from crafts to computer programs

prototype (**PROH**-toh-type) a rough draft of an invention or idea

Find Out More

Books

Fontichiaro, Kristin. *Designing Board Games*. Ann Arbor, MI: Cherry Lake Publishing, 2017.

Petelinsek, Kathleen. *Creating Pipe Cleaner Crafts*. Ann Arbor, MI: Cherry Lake Publishing, 2015.

Web Sites

Imagination Foundation: Global Cardboard Challenge
http://cardboardchallenge.com
Join the Global Cardboard Challenge, where kids build anything they can dream up using cardboard.

Kids Activities Blog: 30 Cardboard Box Crafts
http://kidsactivitiesblog.com/52717/30-cardboard-box-crafts
Get some more ideas for cardboard projects you can build.

Index

About the Author

Amy Quinn is a first-grade teacher in West Bloomfield, Michigan. She is also a coach and mentor for FIRST LEGO League and a team manager for Destination Imagination. Amy has a daughter named Emily and a son named Tommy who both love to design and create new things!